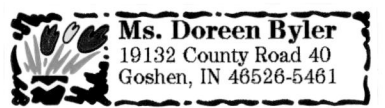
Ms. Doreen Byler
19132 County Road 40
Goshen, IN 46526-5461

Poetry for Young People
Emily Dickinson

Edited by Frances Schoonmaker Bolin
Illustrated by Chi Chung

Sterling Publishing Co., Inc.
New York

Dedication

*To my mother
Aleene Elizabeth Shannon Schoonmaker*

Acknowledgments

Thanks to Nancy D. Lewis and Dorothy Lewis for their many suggestions, and to Mary Sullivan for her assistance.

A MAGNOLIA EDITIONS BOOK

Editors: Karla Olson, Loretta Mowat
Art Director/Designer: Jeff Batzli
Production Manager: Jeanne E. Kaufman

Library of Congress Cataloguing-in-Publication Data
Dickinson, Emily, 1830-1886.
   [Poems. Selections]
   Emily Dickinson : poetry for young people / edited by
Frances S. Bolin ; illustrated by Chi Chung.
      p. cm.
   ISBN 0-8069-0635-9
   1. Children's poetry, American. [1. American poetry.]
I. Bolin. Frances S. II. Chung. Chi, ill. III. Title.
PS1541. A1 1994
811'.4--dc20   94-13809
                                                    CIP
                                                    AC

8 10 9

Published by Sterling Publishing Company, Inc.
387 Park Avenue South, New York, N.Y. 10016

©1994 by Magnolia Editions Limited
Introduction © 1994 Francis Schoonmaker Bolin
Illustration © 1994 Chi Chung
Photography p.4: Amherst College Library

Distributed in Canada by Sterling Publishing
c/o Canadian Manda Group, One Atlantic Avenue, Suite 105
Toronto, Ontario, Canada M6K 3E7
Distributed in Great Britain and Europe by Cassell PLC
Villiers House, 41/47 Strand, London WC2N 5JE, England
Distributed in Australia by Capricorn Link (Australia) Pty Ltd.
P.O. Box 6651, Baulkham Hills, Business Centre,
NSW 2153, Australia

"I dwell in Possibility," from THE COMPLETE POEMS OF
EMILY DICKINSON, edited by Thomas H. Johnson.
Copyright 1929 by Martha Dickinson Bianchi:
Copyright renewed 1957 by Mary L. Hampson. Reprinted by
permission of Little, Brown and Company.

"Bee, I'm expecting you!" and "A soft sea washed around the
house" from BOLTS OF MELODY:New Poems of Emily
Dickinson by Millicent Todd Bingham. Copyright 1945 by
Millicent Todd Bingham. Copyright renewed 1973 by
Katherine Loomis and George Loomis II. Reprinted by
permission of HarperCollins Publishers, Inc.

Printed in China
All rights reserved

Sterling ISBN 0-8069-0635-9

Contents

Introduction 4

Hope is the thing with feathers 8

It's all I have to bring today 9

I started early, took my dog 11

I'm nobody! Who are you? 12

I hide myself within my flower 14

I dwell in Possibility 14

Will there really be a morning? 15

I'll tell you how the sun rose 16

She sweeps with many-colored brooms 17

I know some lonely houses off the road 18

The moon was but a chin of gold 20

Pink, small, and punctual 21

His bill an auger is 22

An everywhere of silver 23

I like to see it lap the miles 24

A fuzzy fellow without feet 26

It sifts from leaden sieves 27

A narrow fellow in the grass 29

Dear March, come in! 30

Bee, I'm expecting you! 31

The grass so little has to do 32

A bird came down the walk 33

The bee is not afraid of me 34

A soft sea washed around the house 36

To make a prairie it takes a clover and one bee 36

The pedigree of honey 37

Forbidden fruit a flavor has 37

The wind begun to rock the grass 39

The morns are meeker than they were 40

I have not told my garden yet 41

My river runs to thee 42

I never saw a moor 43

There is no frigate like a book 44

If I can stop one heart from breaking 46

A word is dead 47

In this short life 47

Bibliography 48

Index 48

Introduction

"Hope is the thing with feathers," wrote Emily Dickinson. She wrote about hope, as well as flowers, birds, people, life, and death—ordinary things. But she had such a vivid imagination that she seemed to get inside these things and look at them in a new way.

Because she had imagination, Emily could write about places she had never been and things she had never seen. Once she wrote (see page 43):

> I never saw a moor,
> I never saw the sea,
> Yet know I how the heather looks,
> And what a wave must be.

In her mind, Emily could walk her dog, Carlo, along a little path, and visit—not the neighbors, but the sea. Sailing ships, or frigates, were on the upper floor and mermaids came up from the basement, as if the sea were a big house. The sea acted as if it would eat her up. It filled her shoes and followed her all the way to town (see page 11). In her imagintion, Emily travelled all over the world.

When Emily was a girl, almost everyone in Amherst, Massachusetts, knew the Dickinsons. Her grandfather helped to found Amherst College, and her father, Edward, a lawyer, was the treasurer of the college. Edward was a very proper and religious man. Every morning and evening, he read to the family from the Bible and led them in prayer. Every Sunday the family went to the Congregational church. Edward Dickinson also served as United States congressman from Massachusetts for a short time. He was so well known that people called him "Squire" Dickinson.

Emily's mother, Emily Norcross Dickinson, was known for her fine cooking. Austin, Emily's brother, was three years older and known for being very bright. He became a lawyer and the treasurer of Amherst College, just like his father. Her sister, Lavinia, whom everyone called Vinnie, was known to be outspoken and witty. She was also much prettier than Emily.

In such an important family, Emily may have seemed to some like a real "nobody." But inside she knew she was somebody special. She played with this thought in "I'm nobody! Who are you?" (see page 12) and at another time told her brother that "bigness" does not come from outside a person, but is something inside.

In many ways, Emily was much like other girls. She enjoyed simple pleasures, such as parties and social and church activities. She liked to gather flowers in the hills with friends, and collected and pressed the flowers. (Once she told her brother that she knew where all the best flowers were, as if each had a house number.) She kept the family garden and loved to plant wildflowers along with the garden flowers. With such ordinary ways, no one suspected that one day she would be the most famous person from Amherst.

Emily loved school, but when she was old enough to attend Amherst Academy, she felt too shy to go alone. She begged her parents to let Vinnie go, too, although Vinnie was much younger. Emily argued that she had been teaching Vinnie to read and that Vinnie was better at arithmetic than she was.

Emily never outgrew this shyness. She was shy around strangers, but when she got to know them, she was witty and fun to be with. People who knew her were also able to accept the odd things she sometimes did, such as the time when she hid from a train. Her father had worked to get the railroad to build a track through Amherst, and everyone in town was excited to see the train make its first trip. Emily, however, hid in the woods where she could watch without being seen!

Perhaps Emily got some of her odd and unpredictable ways, as well as her vision of ordinary things as beautiful and wonderful, from her father. Edward once rang the church bells to call everyone in town out to see a spectacular sunset. No one could have imagined the dignified Edward Dickinson doing such a thing.

Emily began to write poetry when she was in her teens. Nobody in her family was especially interested in writing. But Emily wrote anyway, jotting little notes and verses, particularly Valentine messages. At seventeen, Emily went away to Mount Holyoke Seminary for a year. She was very homesick and wrote many letters home. Austin wrote her back and his letters always cheered her.

It was Austin who wrote Emily about Benjamin Newton, a law student studying with her father. When Emily returned home, she and Ben became good friends, discussing books that Ben loaned to her. Emily's father did not approve of Ben's books, for he felt they contained too many new, liberal ideas. So, to avoid arguments, Ben hid the books in the bushes near the front door when he came to call, and later Emily or Austin collected them.

When Ben left Amherst, he and Emily wrote to each other. Ben was one of the few people who showed an interest in Emily's poetry. He wrote in her autograph album, "All can write autographs, but few paragraphs...."

Not many years later, Benjamin died. Emily was so shocked and sad that she could hardly believe it was true. Sometime later, she began to write poems about death, a part of life that Emily wondered and wrote about for the rest of her life. In "I have not told my garden yet" (see page 41), she imagines her own death.

In Emily's time, people thought that marriage offered the best prospects for a woman. Many young men enjoyed Emily's and Vinnie's company, but neither of the sisters ever married. Some people thought that Emily was too free-spirited to marry.

Austin got married and built a house next door. But unmarried young women generally lived at home in those days. Emily continued to tend the garden and became a good cook, like her mother. Her father refused to eat bread baked by anyone else. But Emily hated housecleaning, so Vinnie performed those tasks and left the kitchen to Emily.

In the evenings, Emily practiced the piano or read. Her nose was in a book almost every spare moment. She often said that books were the best company. A book can "take us lands away," she wrote (see page 44).

Emily continued to be very shy. As she grew older, she began to spend less and less time in town, and by the time she was forty, she almost never left home. The only place she went was next door to see Austin and his wife, Sue, always by the little path through the backyard. She hardly saw anyone except her family and some neighborhood children. When friends and neighbors came to call she stayed in her room upstairs. But she always kept her door open so she could hear what was going on. It was around this time that she started to wear only white.

The more Emily stayed by herself, the more curious people in town became about her. Some made up stories about Emily to explain her odd ways. Others came to the door with little gifts just to see if they could get a glimpse of Emily. But Emily saw only those she chose to see. Vinnie always talked to visitors, but protected Emily from the curious. The family did not understand Emily's need to be away from the world, but they respected her wishes.

Her nieces and nephews and the neighborhood children didn't seem to mind that Emily was different. They loved to play in her yard. Sometimes she worked in the garden and watched them from there or the window. When Emily waved her arms to signal, play stopped. Then she would open the window and lower a basket, filled with warm gingerbread, cookies, or raisins, by a knotted cord. Her nephew Ned called Emily his best friend. And once, when her niece, Mattie, was angry with a playmate, Mattie yelled the worst thing she could think of: "You haven't got an Aunt Emily!"

Over the years Emily taught herself to write poetry by writing and writing and writing. After most people had gone to bed, Emily sat up writing. Emily wrote extraordinary things; she lived "in Possibility." Sunrises, sunsets, the moon, shadows on the lawn, storms, and bees were in her poems. But the sun didn't just rise; it rose "a ribbon at a time." The moon could show "a chin of gold," or slide down a chair. A sunset wasn't just pretty colors; it was a woman sweeping with many brooms, each a different color that left a few shreds, or straws, behind. Hills could untie bonnets. With Emily's imagination, lightning displayed a yellow beak and ugly blue claws. A maple tree wore a gay scarf. Birds didn't fly; they unrolled their feathers and rowed home. Her poems about flowers, butterflies, and bees reveal the delight she took in nature and her keen sense of the funny side of things. A good example is her letter from Fly to Bee (see page 31).

Only six of Emily's poems were published while she was alive. Her poems were unusual, not what people seemed to like at the time. Poetry in those days was serious and often used "flowery" language. Emily's was light and witty.

She almost always wrote in a rhythm or meter called iambic. It is supposed to be most like ordinary speech, and is the rhythm used in many of the hymns Emily sang in church. A short syllable is followed by a long one. You can usually clap the rhythm of her poems. The first clap is soft, or weak, and the second loud, or strong. Turn to the poem on page 20 and try it.

Her poems often have stanzas of four lines. In these poems, lines one and three have eight syllables, lines two and four have six syllables, and the last word in line two rhymes with the last word in line four. For an example, see the poem on page 34 entitled "The bee is not afraid of me." Most of her poems have two stanzas, but sometimes there are more; in these poems, each stanza follows the pattern set in the first stanza.

Writing a poem according to these rules is like working out a puzzle. Emily would think of what she wanted to say, then work until it fit the pattern. She always kept a dictionary beside her so she could find a word that would say exactly what she wanted. Many times she marked through a word and replaced it with another. Sometimes she broke the "rules" to include a word that didn't quite fit or to play with an idea in a different way. People were shocked by this, for it was not what they expected.

Almost every evening, Emily sent a note, and often a poem, to Austin's wife, Sue, such as "The morns are meeker than they were" on page 40. Like Ben Newton, Sue was interested in Emily's poetry, although not even Sue knew how much Emily had written. After Emily died at age fifty-five, Vinnie went into her room. To Vinnie's great surprise, she found in the bottom drawer of Emily's bureau a box of little books, each sewn together by hand. There were 879 poems in the little books. Later, more poems were found, for odd little Emily had written more than seventeen hundred poems!

Why did she write? We may never know for certain. But we do know this; Emily Dickinson chose to spend day after day in the same house, doing the same things—ordinary, seemingly unimportant things—for she seemed to know that there are wonderful possibilities in the most ordinary life if we just take notice.

Emily wrote in a letter, "To live is so startling it leaves little time for anything else." Living, thinking, and imagining were a full-time job to Emily Dickinson. She believed that feelings are to be thought about, not put aside. Perhaps she wrote to capture what she noticed, what she imagined, and how she felt.

Hope is the thing with feathers
That perches in the soul,
And sings the tune without the words,
And never stops at all,

And sweetest in the gale is heard;
And sore must be the storm
That could abash the little bird
That kept so many warm.

I've heard it in the chillest land,
And on the strangest sea;
Yet, never, in extremity,
It asked a crumb of me.

gale—*a strong wind*
abash—*to astonish; to make feel ill at ease or self-conscious*
extremity—*a most difficult or dangerous time or situation*

It's all I have to bring today,
    This, and my heart beside,
This, and my heart, and all the fields,
    And all the meadows wide.
Be sure you count, should I forget—
    Some one the sum could tell—
This, and my heart, and all the bees
    Which in the clover dwell.

I started early, took my dog,
And visited the sea—
The mermaids in the basement
Came out to look at me,

And frigates in the upper floor
Extended hempen hands—
Presuming me to be a mouse
Aground, upon the sands,

But no man moved me till the tide
Went past my simple shoe—
And past my apron and my belt,
And past my bodice too,

And made as he would eat me up
And wholly as a dew
Upon a dandelion's sleeve—
And then I started too.

And he—he followed close behind;
I felt his silver heel
Upon my ankle—then my shoes
Would overflow with pearl.

Until we met the solid town,
No one he seemed to know—
And bowing with a mighty look
At me, the sea withdrew.

frigates—*medium-sized warships with sails*
hempen—*ropelike (some rope is made from hemp, which is a
     plant with tough fiber in its stem)*
bodice—*the part of a woman's dress above the waist*

I'm nobody! Who are you?
Are you nobody, too?
Then there's a pair of us—don't tell!
They'd banish us, you know.

How dreary to be somebody!
How public, like a frog
To tell your name the livelong day
To an admiring bog!

banish—*to send away or get rid of*
bog—*wet, marshy ground*

I hide myself within my flower,
That wearing on your breast
You, unsuspecting, wear me too—
And angels know the rest.

I hide myself within my flower,
That fading from your vase,
You, unsuspecting, feel for me
Almost a loneliness.

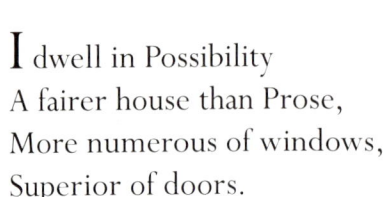

I dwell in Possibility
A fairer house than Prose,
More numerous of windows,
Superior of doors.

Of chambers, as the cedars—
Impregnable of eye;
And for an everlasting roof
The gables of the sky.

Of visitors—the fairest—
For occupation—this—
The spreading wide my narrow hands
To gather Paradise.

impregnable—*can't be captured; unshakable*

Will there really be a morning?
Is there such a thing as day?
Could I see it from the mountains
If I were as tall as they?

Has it feet like water-lilies?
Has it feathers like a bird?
Is it brought from famous countries
Of which I have never heard?

Oh, some scholar! Oh, some sailor!
Oh, some wise man from the skies!
Please to tell a little pilgrim
Where the place called morning lies!

I'll tell you how the sun rose,—
A ribbon at a time.
The steeples swam in amethyst,
The news like squirrels ran.

The hills untied their bonnets,
The bobolinks begun.
Then I said softly to myself,
"That must have been the sun!"

But how he set I know not.
There seemed a purple stile
Which little yellow boys and girls
Were climbing all the while

Till when they reached the other side,
A dominie in gray
Put gently up the evening bars,
And led the flock away.

amethyst—*purple or violet color; a kind of quartz used in jewelry*
bobolinks—*songbirds that live in fields and meadows*
stile—*a set of steps used for climbing over a fence or wall*
dominie—*a pastor or member of the clergy; in Scotland, a schoolmaster*

She sweeps with many-colored brooms,
And leaves the shreds behind;
Oh, housewife in the evening west,
Come back, and dust the pond!

You dropped a purple ravelling in,
You dropped an amber thread;
And now you've littered all the East
With duds of emerald!

And still she plies her spotted brooms,
And still the aprons fly,
Till brooms fade softly into stars—
And then I come away.

ravelling—*a thread that has been pulled from a woven cloth*
plies—*uses energetically*

I know some lonely houses off the road
A robber'd like the look of.—
Wooden-barred,
And windows hanging low,
Inviting to
A portico,
Where two could creep:
One hand the tools,
The other peep
To make sure all's asleep.
Old-fashioned eyes,
Not easy to surprise!

How orderly the kitchen'd look by night,
With just a clock,—
But they could gag the tick,
And mice won't bark;
And so the walls don't tell,
None will.

A pair of spectacles ajar just stir—
An almanac's aware.
Was it the mat winked,
Or a nervous star?
The moon slides down the stair
To see who's there.

18

There's plunder,—where?
Tankard, or spoon,
Earring, or stone,
A watch, some ancient brooch
To match the grandmamma,
Staid sleeping there.

Day rattles, too,
Stealth's slow;
The sun has got as far
As the third sycamore.
Screams chanticleer,
"Who's there?"
And echoes, trains away,
Sneer—"Where?"
While the old couple, just astir,
Fancy the sunrise left the door ajar!

portico—*a porch or covered walk that has a roof supported by columns; often at the entrance to a building*
plunder—*a stolen item*
stealth—*secret, sly action*
chanticleer—*an ancient name for a rooster*

The moon was but a chin of gold
    A night or two ago,
And now she turns her perfect face
    Upon the world below.

Her forehead is of amplest blonde,
    Her cheek like beryl stone,
Her eye unto the summer dew
    The likest I have known.

Her lips of amber never part,
    But what must be the smile
Upon her friend she could bestow,
    Were such her silver will.

And what a privilege to be
    But the remotest star.
For certainly her way might pass
    Beside your twinkling door.

Her bonnet is the firmament,
    The universe her shoe,
The stars the trinkets at her belt,
    Her dimities of blue.

THE NEXT SEVEN POEMS ARE RIDDLES EMILY WROTE. SEE IF YOU CAN GUESS WHAT SHE IS DESCRIBING. THE ANSWERS ARE UPSIDE DOWN AT THE END OF EACH POEM, BUT DON'T PEEK UNTIL YOU'VE TRIED TO SOLVE THE RIDDLES. YOU MAY WANT TO COVER THE PICTURES, TOO.

Pink, small, and punctual
Aromatic, low,
Covert in April,
Candid in May,

Dear to the moss,
Known by the knoll,
Next to the robin
In every human soul,

Bold little beauty,
Bedecked with thee,
Nature forswears Antiquity.

covert—*hidden or disguised*
knoll—*a little hill or mound*

(an arbutus, a plant with little pink or white blossoms and strawberry-like berries)

His bill an auger is,
   His head, a cap and frill.
He laboreth at every tree,—
   A worm his utmost goal.

auger—*a tool for drilling holes in wood*

(a woodpecker)

An everywhere of silver,
With ropes of sand
To keep it from effacing
The track called land.

effacing—*wiping out or erasing something*

(the sea)

I like to see it lap the miles,
And lick the valleys up,
And stop to feed itself at tanks;
And then, prodigious, step

Around a pile of mountains,
And, supercilious, peer
In shanties by the sides of roads;
And then a quarry pare

To fit its sides, and crawl between,
Complaining all the while
In horrid, hooting stanza;
Then chase itself down hill

And neigh like Boanerges;
Then, punctual as a star,
Stop—docile and omnipotent—
At its own stable door.

prodigious—*amazing; of great size and power*
supercilious—*haughty or proud*
shanties—*small, shabby huts or houses*
quarry—*a place where stone or marble used for building is cut or blasted out of the ground*
Boanerges—*the Apostles James and John, who were called the "Sons of Thunder" because they wanted to call down fire from heaven on the Samaritans (see Mark 3:17)*
omnipotent—*all-powerful*

(a train)

A fuzzy fellow without feet
Yet doth exceeding run!
Of velvet is his countenance
And his complexion dun.

Sometimes he dwelleth in the grass,
Sometimes upon a bough
From which he doth descend in plush
Upon the passer-by.

dun—*a dull grayish brown*

(a caterpillar who becomes a butterfly)

It sifts from leaden sieves,
It powders all the wood,
It fills with alabaster wool
The wrinkles of the road.

It makes an even face
Of mountain and of plain,—
Unbroken forehead from the east
Unto the east again.

It reaches to the fence,
It wraps it, rail by rail,
Till it is lost in fleeces;
It flings a crystal veil

On stump and stack and stem,—
The summer's empty room,
Acres of seams where harvests were,
Recordless, but for them.

It ruffles wrists of posts,
And ankles of a queen,—
Then stills its artisans like ghosts,
Denying they have been.

(Mous)

sieves—*strainers or sifters*
artisans—*skilled workers or craftspeople who make things that show imagination and feeling*

A narrow fellow in the grass
Occasionally rides;
You may have met him,—did you not,
His notice sudden is.

The grass divides as with a comb,
A spotted shaft is seen;
And then it closes at your feet
And opens further on.

He likes a boggy acre,
A floor to cool for corn.
Yet when a child, and barefoot,
I more than once, at morn,

Have passed, I thought, a whip-lash
Unbraiding in the sun,—
When, stooping to secure it,
It wrinkled, and was gone.

Several of nature's people
I know, and they know me;
I feel for them a transport
Of cordiality;

But never met this fellow,
Attended or alone,
Without a tighter breathing,
And zero at the bone.

(a snake)

Dear March, come in!
How glad I am!
I looked for you before.
Put down your hat—
You must have walked—
How out of breath you are!
Dear March, how are you?
And the rest?
Did you leave Nature well?
Oh, March, come right upstairs with me,
I have so much to tell!

I got your letter, and the birds'—
The maples never knew
That you were coming—I declare,
How red their faces grew!
But, March, forgive me—
And all those hills
You left for me to hue—
There was no purple suitable,
You took it all with you.

Who knocks? That April!
Lock the door!
I will not be pursued!
He stayed away a year, to call
When I am occupied.
But trifles look so trivial
As soon as you have come,
That blame is just as dear as praise
And praise as mere as blame.

hue—*a particular color or tint*
    (Emily is saying, "You left
      it up to me to put the color in!")

A soft sea washed around the house,
A sea of summer air,
And rose and fell the magic planks
That sailed without a care.

For captain was the butterfly,
For helmsman was the bee,
And an entire universe
For the delighted crew.

To make a prairie it takes a clover and one bee—
One clover, and a bee,
And revery.
The revery alone will do
If bees are few.

revery—*dreamy thinking; a state in which
one imagines pleasant things*

The pedigree of honey
Does not conern the bee—
A clover, any time to him
Is aristocracy.

Forbidden fruit a flavor has
    That lawful orchards mocks;
How luscious lies the pea within
    The pod that Duty locks!

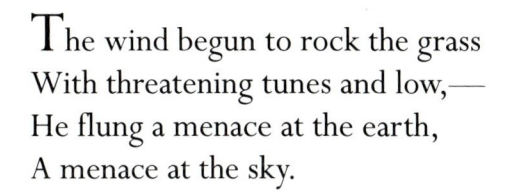

The wind begun to rock the grass
With threatening tunes and low,—
He flung a menace at the earth,
A menace at the sky.

The leaves unhooked themselves from trees
And started all abroad;
The dust did scoop itself like hands
And throw away the road.

The wagons quickened on the streets,
The thunder hurried slow;
The lightning showed a yellow beak,
And then a livid claw.

The birds put up the bars to nests,
The cattle fled to barns;
There came one drop of giant rain,
And then, as if the hands

That held the dams had parted hold,
The waters wrecked the sky,
But overlooked my father's house,
Just quartering a tree.

livid—*having a bluish color; black-and-blue;
discolored by a bruise*

The morns are meeker than they were,
The nuts are getting brown;
The berry's cheek is plumper,
The rose is out of town.

The maple wears a gayer scarf,
The field a scarlet gown.
Lest I should be old-fashioned,
I'll put a trinket on.

I have not told my garden yet,
Lest that should conquer me;
I have not quite the strength now
To break it to the bee.

I will not name it in the street,
For shops would stare, that I,
So shy, so very ignorant,
Should have the face to die.

The hillsides must not know it,
Where I have rambled so,
Nor tell the loving forests
The day that I shall go,

Nor lisp it at the table,
Nor heedless by the way
Hint that within the riddle
One will walk to-day!

My river runs to thee—
Blue sea, wilt welcome me?

My river waits reply.
Oh sea, look graciously!

I'll fetch thee brooks
From spotted nooks—

Say, sea,
Take me!

I never saw a moor,
I never saw the sea,
Yet know I how the heather looks,
And what a wave must be.

I never spoke with God,
Nor visited in heaven,
Yet certain am I of the spot
As if the chart were given.

There is no frigate like a book
    To take us lands away,
Nor any coursers like a page
    Of prancing poetry.
This traverse may the poorest take
    Without oppress of toll;
How frugal is the chariot
    That bears a human soul!

frigate—*a medium-sized warship with sails*
coursers—*graceful, swift horses or runners*

If I can stop one heart from breaking,
I shall not live in vain;
If I can ease one life the aching,
Or cool one pain,
Or help one fainting robin
Unto his nest again,
I shall not live in vain.

A word is dead
When it is said,
    Some say.
I say it just
Begins to live
    That day.

In this short life
That only lasts an hour,
How much, how little,
Is within our power!

Bibliography

Bianchi, Martha Dickinson. *Emily Dickinson Face to Face: Unpublished Letters With Notes and Reminiscences.* Boston: Houghton Mifflin Co., 1932.

Emily Dickinson: A Letter to the World. Chosen and introduced by Rumer Godden. New York: Macmillan, 1968.

Fischer, Aileen, and Olive Rabe. *We Dickinsons: The Life of Emily Dickinson As Seen Through the Eyes of Her Brother Austin.* New York: Athenum, 1965.

Hampson, Alfred Leete, ed. *Emily Dickinson: Poems for Youth.* Foreword by May Lamberton Becker. Boston: Little, Brown and Co., 1934.

I'm Nobody! Who are You? Poems of Emily Dickinson for Children. Introduction by Richard B. Sewall. Owings Mills, Md.: Stemmer House, 1978.

Longsworth, Polly. *Emily Dickinson: Her Letter to the World.* New York: Thomas Y. Crowell Co., 1965.

Poems of Emily Dickinson. Selected by Helen Plotz. New York: Thomas Y. Crowell Co., 1964.

Todd, Mabel Loomis, and Millicent Todd Bingham, eds. *Bolts of Melody: New Poems of Emily Dickinson.* New York: Harper and Brothers Publishers, 1945.

Index

A
Amherst College, 4

B
"Bee, I'm expecting you!," 6, 31
"The bee is not afraid of me," 6, 34
"A bird came down the walk," 33

D
"Dear March, come in!," 30
Dickinson, Emily
    education, 5
    family, 4-6
    interests, 4
    writing style, 5, 6-7

E
"An everywhere of silver," 23

F
"Forbidden fruit a flavor has," 37
"A fuzzy fellow without feet," 26

G
"The grass so little has to do," 32

H
"His bill an auger is," 22
"Hope is the thing with feathers," 4, 8

I
Iambic meter, 6
"I dwell in Possibility," 14
"If I can stop one heart from breaking," 46
"I have not told my garden yet," 5, 40
"I hide myself within my flower," 14
"I know some lonely houses off the road," 18-19
"I like to see it lap the miles," 24
"I'll tell you how the sun rose," 16
"I'm nobody! Who are you?," 4, 12
"I never saw a moor," 4, 43
"I started early, took my dog," 4, 11
"It's all I have to bring today," 9
"It sifts from leaden sieves," 27

M
"The moon was but a chin of gold," 20
"The morns are meeker than they were," 7, 40
"My river runs to thee," 42

N
"A narrow fellow in the grass," 29

P
"The pedigree of honey," 37
"Pink, small, and punctual," 21

S
"She sweeps with many-colored brooms," 17
"A soft sea washed around the house," 36

T
"There is no frigate like a book," 5, 44
"To make a prairie it takes a clover and one bee," 36

W
"Will there really be a morning?," 15
"The wind begun to rock the grass," 39
"A word is dead," 47